...and she sparkled

written by Joan Steffend

illustrated by Fredrick Haugen

TRISTAN PUBLISHING
Minneapolis

To my family,

and all of us who know

there's something more to life.

—Joan

Library of Congress Cataloging-in-Publication Data

Steffend, Joan, 1955-
 And she sparkled / written by Joan Steffend ; illustrated by Fredrick Haugen.
   p. cm.
 ISBN 978-0-931674-83-9 (alk. paper)
 1. Self-realization in women--Fiction. 1. Title.
 PS3619.T4475A85 2010
 813'.6--dc22

                    2010012031

TRISTAN Publishing
2355 Louisiana Avenue North
Golden Valley, MN 55427

Copyright © 2010, Joan Steffend
ISBN 978-0-931674-83-9
Printed in China
Second Printing

Please visit www.tristanpublishing.com

There once was a little girl...

...and she sparkled.

She lived in her magnificence,
singing and dancing wherever life took her.

In the morning,
a finger of sunlight
would reach gently through the blinds
to tickle her awake,

and she would *leap* from her bed,
looking for joy wherever she could find it.

And she found it—with her toes in the grass,
her tiny hands around a dandelion,
her hair tangled from the possibilities for fun
that swirled around her.

She was enough.

At night,
she would snuggle under her covers,
barely able to wait for the dreams
that would take her to even greater places
and set the stage for the next day.

One morning, though,
the sunlight felt sharp

                      stabbing at sleepy eyes.

A little grumble escaped her mouth
as she stumbled out of bed.

She did dance that day, but not as joyfully...

not as she had the day before.

And that night,
she punched at her pillow,
waiting for sleep to take her away from the day.

Away.

Slowly,
the people around her noted with pride
that the little girl was
growing up.
Learning to act 'mature' is what they called it.

They were doing their jobs well.

And so the little girl
became a big girl,
nicely folding her hands in her lap
as she sat very still...

wondering why she felt so alone.

There was still a part of her
that felt like dancing and singing,
but that wasn't acceptable most of the time.

It might disturb someone.
It might not be appropriate.
It most certainly wasn't useful.

So, as the girl grew,
she would lock the door of her room
when the others left and sing and dance
and 'visit' the little girl inside...

being careful to be a little quiet,
so she could hear if anyone returned.

The girl grew and became ever more dutiful.

No one saw her dance.
No one heard her sing.
She memorized the answers others gave her
for who she was...

and soon... it seemed...
even she forgot her little girl.

To be sure, there were days,
when it looked as though the girl was happy,

but the smiles were usually
on the outside,

and not the inside.

Life went on for the girl—now a woman
And her life looked a lot like everyone else's.

She was told *that* was success.

"Life," they said, "is all about fitting in.

Don't ask questions.
It makes us all a little uncomfortable,
and you don't want that."

So the woman spent her days waking up...

and waiting to fall asleep.

She wasn't aware the little girl
was patiently waiting for her...

reaching out in small ways
every day and every night.

But one morning,
she felt a familiar tickle.
The sunlight played on her face for a moment
and it made her smile.

An energy she hadn't felt in some time
lifted her out of bed.

She sensed something familiar and yet...

somehow, it was new.

That day was more ordinary than not,
but from time to time,
she was filled with hope,
which rose in waves
and then disappeared into the ordinary.

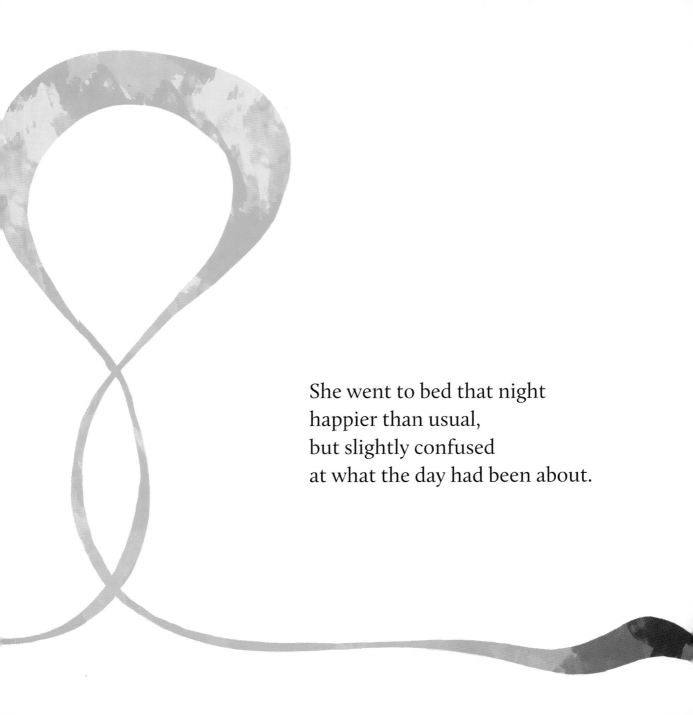

She went to bed that night
happier than usual,
but slightly confused
at what the day had been about.

The next day dawned
and the woman, again, sensed something
familiar and exciting in the sunlight.

In fact, she felt so alive in that moment,
she danced out of bed and down the hall

silently

so no one would hear her.

Moments in the day found her
quietly humming to herself...

dancing in her dreams,
while she lived the life she thought she should.

She went to bed that night,
not as anxious to sleep
as anxious to be awake again.

The months went on that way with joy dancing...
just below the surface of the woman.

As the years went by,
the woman became bolder,
discovering things about herself
she had somehow forgotten.

She spent time every day
hungrily uncovering pieces of a little girl
from long ago.

She decided she could no longer only be
the person others expected to see.

She *was* that, but she was so much more.
She had always been so much more.

She decided to share who she was with the world
and with herself.

There was magic to be remembered...

and there was that urgent and now familiar rhythm
that kept her dancing...

and looking for new songs to sing.

Some people didn't really like that.

They had come to depend on her
the way she used to be.

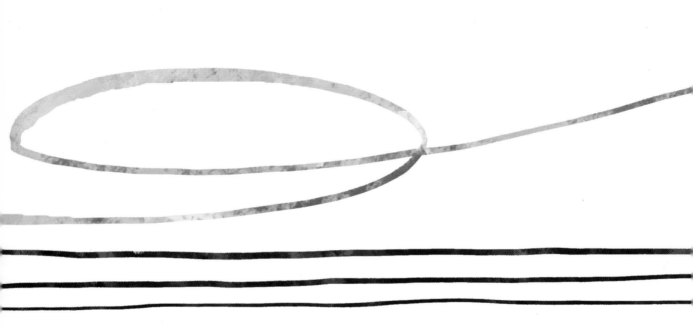

Now she made some of them uncomfortable,
even angry.

"Are people really supposed to listen
to their own rhythm and dance?" they asked.

"Or should they march in the quiet lines
laid out for them?"

It didn't matter to her.
She didn't want to tell anyone else what to do.

The only thing that mattered to the woman
was the voice of the little girl
living in her heart...

whispering softly that she was, indeed, enough.

She was magnificent...

...and she sparkled.

Joan Steffend is a mom, a wife, a TV/radio
host and a lover of people's stories.

For years, she told other people's stories
for a living as a national Emmy-winning
reporter and anchor and then as a host of
HGTV's *Decorating Cents*.

Now she is telling her story, a universal
one of joy lost... and found.

If you are touched by this book, please tell your friends.

www.tristanpublishing.com